A FOREST OF
FAMILY TREES

Miserable Families

Certainly not
for my family...

nor yours

nor mine ...

A FAMILY TREE

FIRST PUBLISHED IN 1995

COPYRIGHT STEVEN APPLEBY © 1995

The moral right of the author has been asserted

BLOOMSBURY PUBLISHING PLC
2 SOHO SQUARE, LONDON W1V 6HB

ISBN 0-7475-2350-9

Printed and bound by the Bath Press

PHOTOGRAPH of Steven Appleby by Pete Bishop

GIVEN TO STAN FOR HIS BIRTHDAY IN JUNE 1996
with love and kisses from Lou

THIS BOOK WOULD NOT HAVE EXISTED WITHOUT:
My family; Pete Bishop; Jonathan Boatfield; Liz Calder;
Jessamy Calkin; Joe Ewart; Malcolm Garrett;
Kasper de Graaf; Matthew Hamilton; Anita Plank;
The Ginger Prince; Nicola Sherring; Howard Trafford;
Noni Ware; Damien Wayling; Janny Kent

SOME OF THESE DRAWINGS HAVE APPEARED IN:
The Guardian; The Sunday Telegraph; Tatler ; Stan's Book

This book is printed entirely on paper
made from family trees

Very rich relative from deported branch of the family.

ASSORTED NAMELESS INDIVIDUALS IN POSITIONS OF AUTHORITY.

No!

No!

No!

No.

Driving examiner.

No!

Bank manager.

No.

No!

Fiancée.

AN EXAMPLE of a TYPICAL EXTENDED FAMILY:

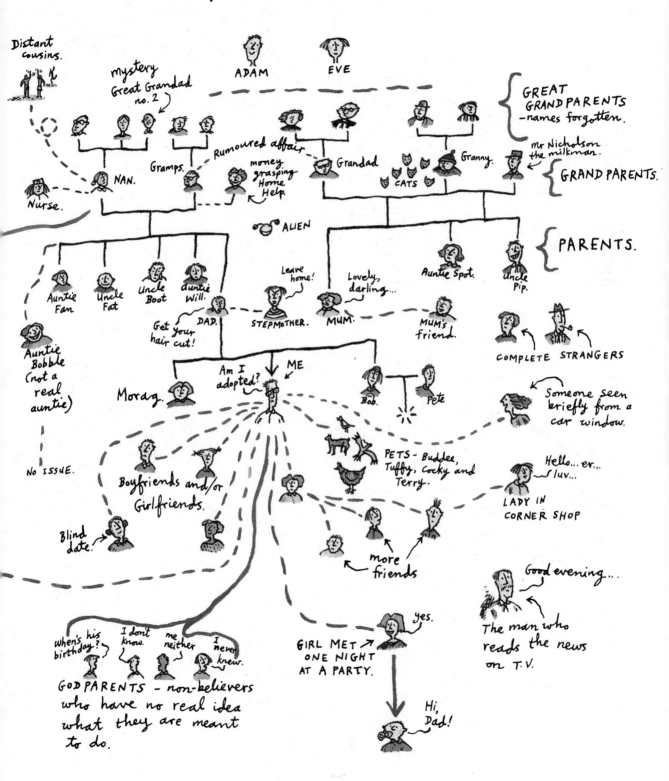

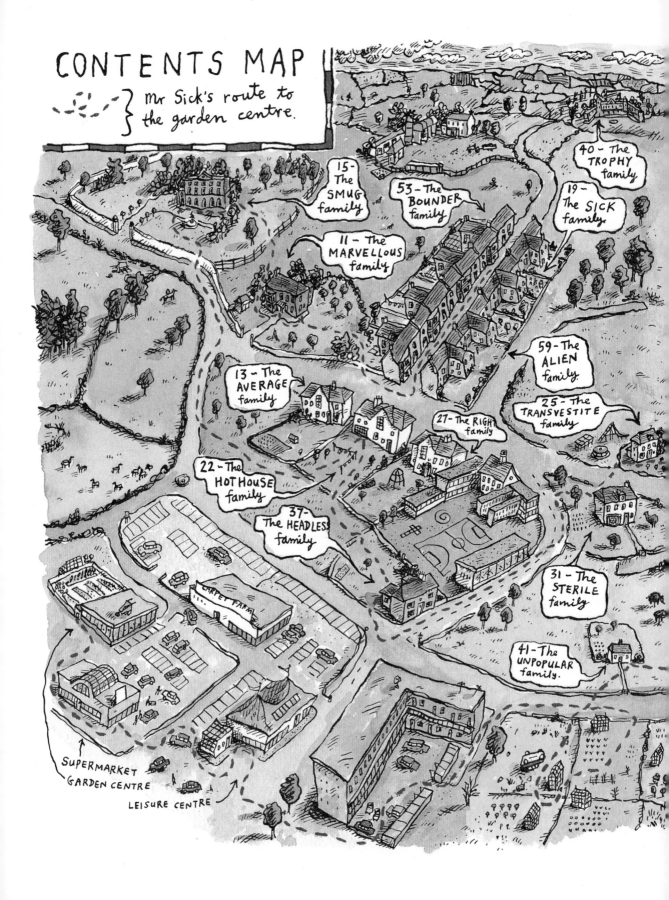

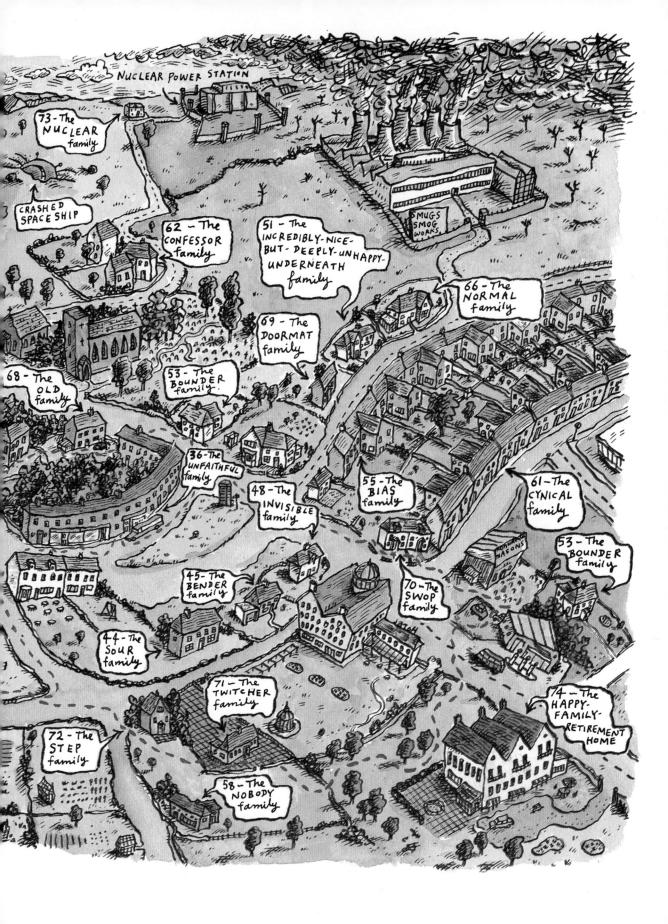

The MARVELLOUS family

The AVERAGE family

MR ANTHONY AVERAGE
the ANT EXPERT

MRS ANDROID AVERAGE
the ANT EXPERT'S WIFE

MISS POPPET AVERAGE
the ANT EXPERT'S
DAUGHTER

MASTER 0·7 AVERAGE
the ANT EXPERT'S SON

An evening with the Averages...

the SMUG family

16

AN AUTHOR RESEARCHING A BOOK:

the lengths you'll go to-----

The SICK family

PETS CORNER

The HOTHOUSE family

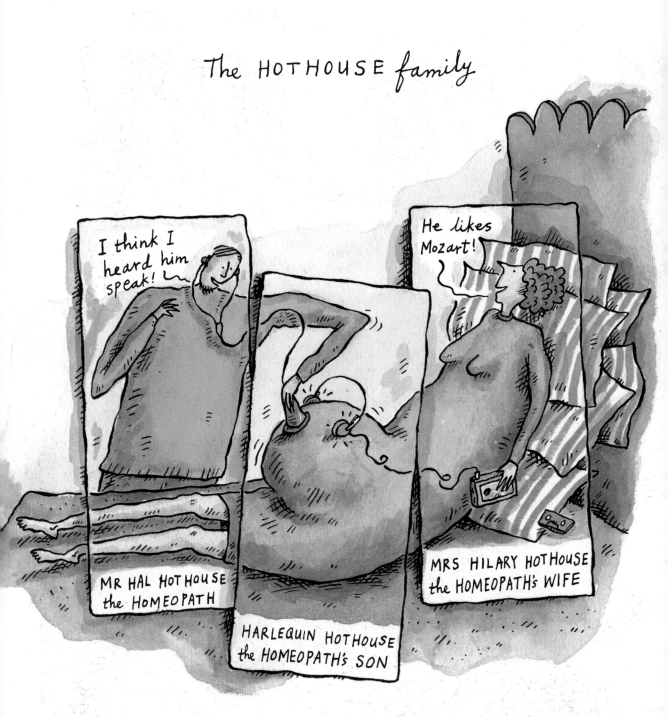

Constructive play fills Harlequin's day.

OTHER THINGS HARLEQUIN CAN SAY:

HARLEQUIN HOTHOUSE ~ A Life...

2 YEARS OLD

I'm testing you, Dad!

10 YEARS OLD

SICK HORROR ALL NIGHT

You never set me any boundaries.

14 YEARS OLD

It's glue, Mum...

Try some.

20 YEARS OLD

Uh... Yeah... uh...

26 YEARS OLD

I've come for the job interview...

32 YEARS OLD

I THINK THEREFORE I AM

I'm teaching Ishmael to read!

The TRANSVESTITE family

Here are the children's dolls:

KENNETH

BARBARA

And the family dog and cat:

Miaow!

Woof!
Woof!

MELK

The RIGHT family

The STERILE family

34

... stan likes to go up ALL the aisles.

The UNFAITHFUL family

MR UTTERLY UNFAITHFUL
the UNDERTAKER

MRS UNBELIEVABLY UNFAITHFUL
the UNDERTAKER'S WIFE

The HEADLESS family

The TROPHY family

The UNPOPULAR family

Party-time at Mr Unpopular's house.

RENTED RELATIVES *

The BENDER family

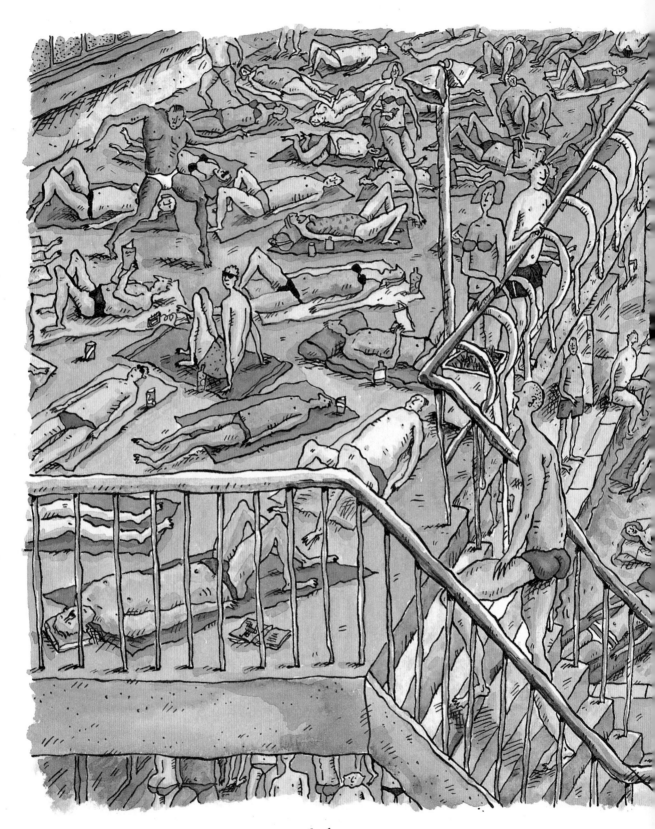

46

let's *not* go here for our holidays!

let's go overland! ♡

The INVISIBLE family

MR INVISIBLE MAN

MRS INVISIBLE MAN

49

Mr Invisible Man at work:

The INCREDIBLY-NICE-BUT-DEEPLY-UNHAPPY-UNDERNEATH family

The CHEESER family

(you fill in the blanks).

The BOUNDER family

Mr Bounder's brother, Bernard, is an airline pilot and an even more successful bigamist.

The BIAS family

The NOBODY family

MR NOBODY

MRS NOBODY

MASTER NOBODY

MISS NOBODY

What luck! An empty compartment

The ALIEN family

The CYNICAL family

Ms. Cynthia Cynical the single mum: "Men! Who needs them!"

Simon Cynical the single mum's son: "I'll be a man one day, Mum." "Get me a drink... NOW!"

Ham, the cynical family's pet hamster

Monty, the cynical family's pet rabbit: "I'm off to get pregnant!"

and you!

The CONFESSOR family

What have you got to confess?!

63

65

The NORMAL family

The OLD family

The DOORMAT family

The SWOP family

The TWITCHER family

All my old toys are still in their boxes...

Never played with...

Worth a lot of money!

MR TWITCHER the TRAIN SPOTTER

I watch soaps on TV...

And I collect soap.

MRS TWITCHER the TRAIN SPOTTER'S WIFE

I collect car registrations and telephone numbers...

Hello?

MASTER TWITCHER the TRAIN SPOTTER'S SON

Wheee... I'm surfing the internet!

MISS TWITCHER the TRAIN SPOTTER'S DAUGHTER

The STEP family

The NUCLEAR family

The ----------- family *

Stick photos here.

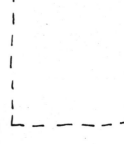

surprise!
(just visiting)

*Insert your own family name in the space provided.

The EXIT family

APPENDICES

a spider

a pruned family tree

THREATS
to family life

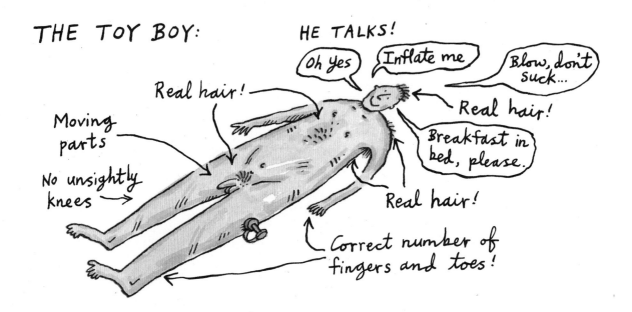

THE TOY GIRL:

THE AU PAIR:

81

THE MILKMAN:

THE POSTMAN:

THE LODGER, or RENT BOY:

HERMAN the HERMAPHRODITE:

CHILDREN:

THE CHILD SNATCHER:

AGEING:

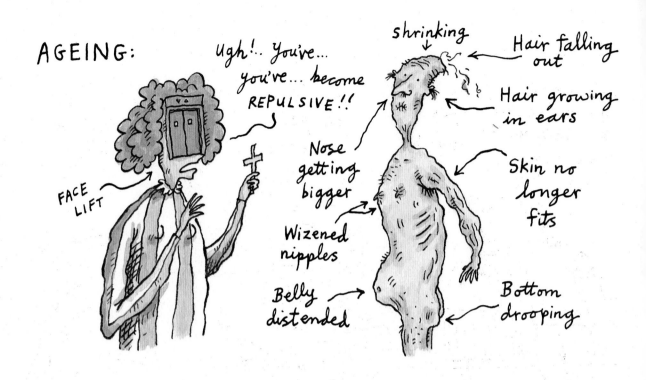

NOT ENOUGH HOURS IN THE DAY:

A momentary magical window of opportunity opens up between the children going to bed and the onset of complete physical exhaustion.

(Know all about this one)

THE AFFAIR!

CRAWLING SKIN:

I'll make a fresh pot.

Don't touch me! You make my skin crawl, going on about tea! You... you... philanderer!

INABILITY TO SLEEP:

I've drunk too much tea.

Me too.

RECONCILIATION:

Z z z z z z z z

Z z z z z z z z

TEAS MAID

89

Yet More
THREATS TO FAMILY LIFE

I'm sure we could think of a few!

TOO-TIRED-TO-THINK:

Darling, I want to talk about us...

Zzzzzzzzzzz snort... snuffle...

WORKAHOLISM:

Darling, I want to
talk about us...

DEAD:

Darling, I want to
talk about us...

UTTER
SILENCE

91

(Just pretending)

A Guide to the

IDENTIFICATION
and care of
FAMILY TREES

Family Tree
Seed

Family Tree
Seedlings

Pull
it up.

A Family Weed

Happy
New
Year!

A Christmas
Family Tree

Gallows Family
Tree

I have
a
small
family.

Bonsai Family
Tree

A Topiary Family Tree Group.

Working out the age of your family by counting the rings in your family tree:

my! We go a long way back!

USEFUL CHAIRS made from family trees:

STEVEN APPLEBY was born in 1956 and will die in _____. He is one insignificant bough somewhere in the middle foliage of a family tree which will grow and grow until the top reaches the Land of Giants, whereupon the world will end and Steven and his relatives will climb up to the Giant's Land singing songs of praise. Once there they will be fattened, slaughtered and baked one by one in a giant oven. Some will be boiled on the hob, others dipped in flour and deep-fried. The Giants will complain bitterly when eating Steven, saying: "There's no meat on't," and, "Pop another'n in." Similar things will happen to YOU on YOUR family tree – but not for a few hundred years yet...

July 23rd 1995

THE END